Myths of
Russia and the
SLAVS

Anita Dalal

RAINTREE
STECK-VAUGHN
PUBLISHERS

A Harcourt Company

Austin   New York
www.raintreesteckvaughn.com

Steck–Vaughn Company
First published 2002 by Raintree Steck-Vaughn Publishers, an imprint of Steck-Vaughn Company.

© 2002 Brown Partworks Limited

Library of Congress Cataloging-in-Publication Data

Dalal, Anita.
    Myths of Russia and the Slavs / Anita Dalal.
        p. cm. -- (Mythic world)
    Includes bibliographical references and index.
    ISBN 0-7398-4979-4

Printed and bound in the United States
1 2 3 4 5 6 7 8 9 0 IP 05 04 03 02 01

Series Consultant: C. Scott Littleton, Professor of Anthropology,
Occidental College, Los Angeles
Volume Author: Anita Dalal

for Brown Partworks
Project Editor: Lee Stacy
Designer: Sarah Williams
Picture Researcher: Helen Simm
Cartographer: Mark Walker
Indexer: Kay Ollerenshaw
Managing Editor: Tim Cooke
Design Manager: Lynne Ross
Production Manager: Matt Weyland

for Raintree Steck-Vaughn
Project Editor: Sean Dolan
Production Manager: Richard Johnson

Contents

General Introduction

MYTHS ARE THE MIRRORS of humanity. They reflect the inner soul of a culture and try to give profound answers in a seemingly mysterious world. In other words, myths give the relevant culture an understanding of its place in the world and the universe in general. Found in all civilizations, myths sometimes combine fact and fiction and other times are complete fantasy. Regardless of their creative origin, myths are always dramatic.

Every culture has its own myths, yet globally there are common themes and symbols, even across civilizations that had no contact with or awareness of each other. Some of the most common types include those that deal with the creation of the world, the cosmos, or a particular site, like a large mountain or lake.

Other myths deal with the origin of humans, or a specific people, culture, or civilization, or the heroes or gods who either made the world inhabitable or gave humans something essential, such as the ancient Greek Titan Prometheus, who gave fire, or the Ojibwa hero Wunzh, who was given divine instructions on cultivating corn. There are also myths about the end of the world, death and the afterlife, and the renewal or change of seasons.

Right: *An ancient Slavic silver ornament made in the years just before the Slavs converted to Christianity.*

The origin of evil and death are also common themes. Examples of such myths are the Biblical Eve eating the forbidden fruit or the ancient Greek story of Pandora opening the sealed box. Additionally there are flood myths, myths about the sun and the moon, and myths of a peaceful, beautiful place of reward, such as heaven or

Elysium, or of punishment, such as hell or Tartarus. Myths also teach important human values, such as courage. In all cases, myths show that the gods and their deeds are outside of ordinary human life and yet essential to it.

Few Slavic and Russian myths survive; this volume presents some of the best known. It also includes a number of folk tales. Although they are not strictly myths, and do not seek to explain fundamental aspects of life in the way that myths do, they still closely reflect how the Slavs saw themselves and their world. Following each story is an explanation of how it was either reflected in or linked to the real life of the Slavs and Russians. There is also a glossary at the end of the volume to help identify the major mythological and historical characters and explain cultural terms.

MYTHOLOGY OF RUSSIA AND SLAVS

By the time Prince Vladimir I led the conversion of the eastern Slavs to Christianity, in the 10th century, the Slavic peoples had already developed a rich and dramatic body of myths and legends. These ancient stories were rooted in the everyday fears and activities of ordinary Slavs, and in the foreign cultures they encountered.

Two thousand years before Vladimir, some historians believe, the Slavs emerged in an area north of the Carpathian Mountains (see map). Their early myths were concerned with the battle between day and night, good and evil. The contrasts were represented in the gods Byelobog (light and good) and Chernobog (night and evil). When the Slavs migrated to other parts of Europe in the centuries that followed, they took their myths.

The eastern Slavs, the main subject of this volume, lived mostly in small villages of a few families, and they had to face many dangers. In the forests, bears and wolves preyed on livestock and people, and the winters were long and harsh. The

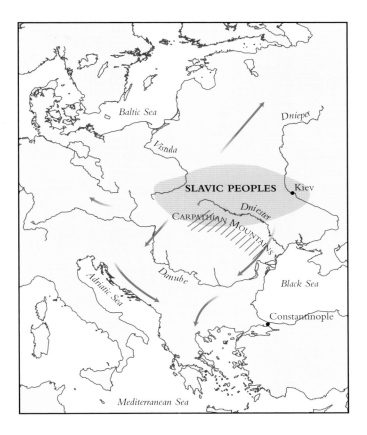

Above: *This map shows the migration routes of the early Slavs as they journeyed from their origins to become the dominant culture in eastern Europe.*

people believed that spirits, some good, some evil, inhabited everything from trees to houses. They also believed in witches, such as Baba Yaga.

The Slavs also had many hero gods. Most of them were adopted from deities of other cultures that the Slavs interacted with. The most important were the Varangians, Vikings who conquered eastern Europe and ruled over the Slavs. For example, the Varangian god Thor became the Slav deity Perun, god of thunder and war.

In medieval times hero knights, called *bogatyri*, took over from the hero gods. These legendary knights, such as Dobrynya and Ilya Muromets, inspired the Slavs with acts of bravery and honor. Around the same time, tales emerged of a new evil creature of the night, the vampire.

The Creation of Mother Russia

This ancient creation myth is eastern Slavic in origin and explains how both the universe and the world were made. In this version Russia is made from the newly created world.

AT THE BEGINNING of time the only thing that existed was darkness. Then the One Who Is Above Everything made a golden egg. Imprisoned inside the golden egg was Rod, who became known as the creator. Rod gave birth to Lada, who was able to crack the golden egg and free Rod. Lada later became the goddess of love and springtime.

After Rod had been freed from the golden egg he used his body to create the universe. From his face he made the sun and from his chest emerged the moon. Stars flew out of his eyes and his eyebrows became the dawn. The dark nights were born from his thoughts and the strong winds that sweep across the earth issued from his breath.

Next Rod separated the physical world from the spiritual world. He then divided the path of Right, known as *Prav*, from the path of Wrong, known as *Yav*, so that they were clearly separated. The creator then forged a fiery chariot, out of which came the thunder that rumbles across the sky. He then put the sun into a golden boat so that it would shine with brilliant golden rays. He also placed the moon in a silver boat so that the moon's rays would appear silver in the night sky.

Rod then turned himself into the river of heaven and created the waters of the Great Ocean. From the foam of the Great Ocean came the World Duck, who went on to make many more gods and demons. Rod also created the cow Zemun and the goat Sedun. From Sedun's breasts came the milk that makes up the Milky Way lighting up the night sky.

Rod then forged the sacred Alatyr Stone and used it to churn butter out of Sedun's breast milk in the Milky Way. It was from this butter that Mother Earth was born, from whom everything good, including Mother Russia (also known as *Rodina*), came to be.

Finally out of his mouth came Bird Mother Sva, who was actually Rod's spirit. Sva soon gave birth to Svarog, who was instantly crowned king of heaven and ruler of all the gods. Svarog also took over the creation of the world from Rod.

Among the many things that King Svarog built were the 12 columns upon which the sky now rests. He lives in the ever-flowing stream that does not freeze in winter, and he continues to watch over the earth and all its creatures. When it pleases him he can bring the dead back to life.

Above: *The milk from the heavenly goat Sedun was churned by the creator god Rod to make the Milky Way, photographed here from earth. Rod used the same butter to make Mother Earth and Mother Russia.*

The Early Slavs and Their History

The precise origin of the Slavs is unknown, but by the 10th century the different Slavic groups together formed the dominant culture in much of central and eastern Europe.

The earliest origins of the Slavs and their myths are shrouded in uncertainty. Although the account of Rod and the creation of the Slav world (see pages 6–7) is ancient, it was not written down until much later because the early Slavs did not have a written language. Instead, the story was passed on from generation to generation by word of mouth. Similarly, the exact origin of the original Slavs remains controversial, but one popular theory holds that they originated in the basins of the Vistula and Upper Dniester rivers just northeast of the Carpathian Mountains (see map on page 5).

Some historians think that the earliest Slavs can be traced back as far as 3,000 years ago (others only trace the origin of the Slavic tribes to the 1st century A.D.) Archaeologists know that there was very early contact between the Slavs and various Iranian tribes — mainly the Scythians and Sarmatians — who traveled as far as present-day Ukraine.

The Slavic language belongs to the Balto-Slavic sub-group of the huge Indo-European language family. But they also borrowed many words from the Iranians. When the Iranian group called the Sarmatians arrived in Slavic territory in the 1st century B.C., the Slavs adopted some of their language and some of their religious practices. For example, the Slavic word for god, *bogu*, is Persian, and the worship of the sun was an Iranian practice that the Slavs adopted in their worship of Dazhbog, the sun god.

Above: *This ritual mask, forged from metal, dates from the 6th century B.C. It comes from an area in the present-day Czech Republic, one of several areas from where archaeologists believe the Slavic peoples might have emerged.*

EXPANDING IN EUROPE

The major expansion of the Slavs took place between the 4th and 6th centuries A.D., when they separated into three major groups that migrated in different directions. The eastern Slavs moved to present-day Ukraine, Belarus, and Russia; the western Slavs comprise present-day Poles, Czechs, Moravians, and Slovaks; and the southern Slavs moved into the Balkans.

Until the 8th century A.D. all the Slavs spoke essentially the same language, with regional dialects. Today there are some 13 Slavic languages. Writing was introduced by Christian missionaries in the 10th century, when the eastern Slavs were forced to convert to Christianity by their ruler, Vladimir I.

The eastern Slavs worshiped nature — particularly the earth, which they thanked for its fertility — and the spirits of the dead. Their chief god was

Left: *For the eastern Slavs who settled in Russia, the forests provided everything from shelter, especially in the long winter months, to food in the form of small game and berries.*

Below: *Many Slavs lived on the Russian steppes, or plains, an area that gave little protection against the elements.*

Perun, the god of lightning, and their ceremonies were performed under oak trees. Later, Dazhbog became the most important god.

The eastern Slavs lived in two very different environments, the steppe (plains) and forest. The people of the steppe were called *Polyáne* and the people of the forest were known as *Drevlyáne*. Kiev, located on the Dnieper River in present-day Ukraine, was the most important settlement and the center of the first Russian state, Kievan Rus. (Scholars believe the Rus — meaning "rowers" — were Vikings, or Varangians, not Slavs; see page 16.) From the 9th to 12th centuries Kiev was one of Europe's most important cities.

Many of the pagan Slavic rituals that structured the daily life of the eastern Slavs, such as folklore, songs, dance, and games, survived into the 20th century because many rural Russians led isolated lives that only began to change radically after the Russian Revolution in 1917.

God Battles Satanail

Many ancient Slavic myths developed over the centuries to include Christian elements. This myth uses the Christian story of the defeat of Satan (called Satanail) by God to provide an explanation for the existence of good and evil.

IN THE BEGINNING God ruled everything but there existed only the light kingdom — heaven — and the dark kingdom — earth. In the light kingdom lived God and all the angels. The mightiest was Satanail, but he was jealous of God and wanted to prove that he was the stronger. One day Satanail tried to push God off his throne. But he failed.

Eventually Satanail left heaven feeling bitter and determined to get his revenge. He flew down to earth, where he walked through mud, which made him stronger. He flew back up to heaven and challenged God again. This time God agreed to a contest. The winner would be the one whom the newly created people would follow.

God allowed Satanail to create the first person. The mighty angel flew down to the dark kingdom, gathered some clay, and made a figure in the image of God. It could not move or do anything, but when God touched the clay figure it came to life. Then God took some more clay and made another person — this time a beautiful girl. Each figure took God's hands and went with him to the heavenly garden.

Satanail decided to steal the people. He snuck into the heavenly garden. The two people were in a fenced-in paradise where God's power prevented Satanail from entering. But Satanail tempted the people over the fence and took them to earth.

When God discovered what had happened he created millions of warriors, more even than the number of stars in heaven. He gave each a sword and led them down to earth. Satanail created more demons than there are grains of sand.

The demons battled the warriors for 77 days. The earth groaned and the heavens shook. Finally, God defeated Satanail and banished him and his demonic force into the darkness. God then found the two people on an island in the middle of an ocean. They begged for God to forgive them and to return them to heaven.

God forgave them but made them stay on earth. He taught them to work and to understand good and evil. God then returned to heaven, where he hung a fiery sword — the sun — above the earth to signal his victory over Satanail. When it shines Satanail is silent, but when night falls on earth he tries to tempt people into performing evil acts.

God Battles Satanail

Left: *From clay God created two figures that became the first people. These figures were tempted out of their refuge by Satanail. This clay statue of a female was molded over 2,000 years ago.*

Good Versus Evil

Long before the Slavs were familiar with the Christian story of God battling Satan, they told tales that expressed the same moral view of good versus evil.

The story of Satanail — or Satan — was a popular Russian folktale that explained the opposition between good and evil (see page 10). This belief in good versus evil became extremely popular in the Slavic world (indeed, throughout the Christian world) in the late 10th century, after Vladimir I had converted Kievan Rus to Christianity in A.D. 988.

About the same time, belief of good versus evil found a strong advocate in a Manichaean Christian sect that began in Bulgaria called the Bogomils. The Bogomils preached about the constant battle between good and evil. This Christian movement also had a profound impact in other parts of Europe, especially southern France, in the 12th century.

ANCIENT SLAVIC BELIEF

Among the Slavs a belief in good versus evil was actually much older than the Bogomils. For the ancient Slavs it lay at the heart of Slavic mythology and was symbolized in the pagan gods, Byelobog and Chernobog.

Below: A Scythian carving of a hero battling a monster — an early example of good versus evil — which dates from the 6th century B.C. The Scythians occupied southern Russia, an area that would become home to the Slavs.

Byelobog was worshiped by Baltic Slavs and Chernobog was his opposite.

Chernobog and Byelobog were two of the earliest gods in the Slavic pantheon. While there are no recorded myths about the battles of the destructive force of Chernobog and Byelobog's creative force, many other things are known about the gods.

Byelobog was the beneficent god of light. The adjective *byely* means white and *bog* means god. Another name for

Byelobog was "Byelun" — the word for paradise. Chernobog, in contrast, was the lord of darkness and evil. *Cherny* means black, and Chernobog was always described as wearing only black. Even today, a common Ukrainian insult is "may the black god exterminate you."

Byelobog was often depicted as an old man with a white beard and white clothing. He only appeared during the day and would help people who were lost in the forests and peasants working in fields.

In contrast, Chernobog appeared only at night. This is because one of the most important of the opposites in Slavic mythology was the contrast between light and dark. The Slavic people thought light was wholesome and understandable, while darkness signified demons, dead people, monsters, and everything that could not be explained and was dangerous.

For the Slavs, the long winter, with its endless dark nights, was something to be endured. The arrival of spring, with its longer days, was celebrated as the time for planting after months of snow. Chernobog's sinister representation signified the dark winter days.

Chernobog was a powerful god. Since he was capable of causing trouble, people tried to keep him happy. Prayers were offered to him during banquets using a round vessel. Prayers were said for Chernobog and Byelobog over the vessel. From Byelobog people expected good events, and while they hoped prayers to Chernobog would prevent misfortune.

Left: *A Slavic shaman performs an ancient pagan ritual. He is surrounded by examples of traditional Slavic nomadic life. His clothes, drum, and tepee are made from animal skins.*

Left: *This painting, titled* Shrovetide, *shows the Russian celebration that marks the end of winter. Shrovetide is a Christian holiday taken from a pagan festival that celebrated the end of Chernobog's winter reign.*

Why the Dnieper Flows So Swiftly

Myths often offer an explanation for the existence of major natural features. This Slavic story tells of the beginning of one of the longest eastern European rivers, the Dnieper.

A LONG TIME AGO, Volga, Dvina, and Dnieper were poor orphans with no one to look after them. They wore rags and were often cold. To feed themselves they had to work hard in the fields, digging and plowing from morning to night. They were very unlucky when it came to farming, and despite working hard they often went to bed hungry.

At the end of one very long day plowing in the fields, Dnieper, who was a boy, sat with his two sisters, Dvina and Volga, on a piece of scrubland by the river. They watched the big, red sun setting the sky alight as it sank toward the distant horizon. The three children were complaining about how hard their life was and how hungry they were. They started to argue about whether they might be able to find an easier way of living.

As they watched the waters flow gently by, the three thought that they might be able to transform themselves into rivers. They decided the only way to do this was to travel the world to try to find a good place to change into rivers.

For three years they wandered the earth until they found a swamp that seemed to be a good place to start three rivers. Having journeyed for so long, the three siblings decided to sleep for the rest of the day and start their new lives as rivers the next morning.

But before they fell asleep Volga and Dvina decided that they wanted to get ahead of their brother. So the sisters waited until they heard Dnieper snoring and then found a gentle incline and started to flow away. When Dnieper awoke the next morning at first he could see no sign of his sisters. Then he saw there were two new rivers and realized that his sisters had tricked him. He was furious and raced alongside the rivers trying to reach their end.

As he ran he realized that it would be much faster to turn himself into a river because no matter how fast he ran he could not beat the fast-flowing rivers that his sisters had become.

Hitting the ground with all his strength he turned into a stream, but he was so angry that his rage sent him tumbling down the steep slopes where rapids formed. When his sisters heard him, they were scared and ran away from each other into the sea. For his part, Dnieper grew calm when he got close to the seashore, and he flowed gently into the waters of the Black Sea.

Above: *By racing so hard to catch up to his sisters, Dnieper turned into a mighty river, which flows some 1,370 miles (2,200 km). This late 19th-century painting shows a calm section of the Dnieper at nighttime.*

The Varangians and Their Slavic Territories

The eastern Slavs who settled in present-day Russia, Ukraine, and Belarus came to be dominated by the Varangians, a group of Vikings who are credited with building Kievan Rus.

The Dnieper River (see map on page 5) played a crucial role in the decision of the Varangians (Vikings who settled in the territories belonging to the eastern Slavs) to take control of present-day European Russia and Ukraine. The river was the main access for the Varangians to the highly prized trading center of Constantinople, the capital of the Byzantine Empire. Also known as Byzantium, the Byzantine Empire was the historical continuation in the east of the ancient Roman Empire. During the 9th and 10th centuries Byzantium was experiencing its wealthiest period.

In around A.D. 862 the Varangians, under the leadership of Prince Rurik of Jutland, took control of Novgorod in northwest Russia. By A.D. 882, three years after Rurik's death, the Varangians, now led by his brother, Oleg, had extended their rule to the strategically important settlements of Kiev and Smolensk. Rurik and his

Left: *A 9th-century Varangian gravestone from Kievan Rus.*

Varangian brothers were also called "Rus," which means "rowers," from which Russia gets its name.

The Varangians played a crucial role in the development of Slavic mythology because they brought with them their gods and beliefs, which fused with those of the eastern Slavs. The clearest example of this is in the appearance of

Perun, the Slavic god of thunder and war, who is similar to Thor, the Viking god of thunder and war (see page 20).

There are different accounts of how the Varangians came to be in the area surrounding Kiev. One version, put forward by the Varangians, is that they were invited by the eastern Slavs to rule.

Above: *A ruler of Byzantium, Theophilus, is flanked by two Varangian guards.*

According to Varangian chronicles, the eastern Slavs were not unified and there was much infighting. Eventually they realized they could not govern themselves and needed the type of firm leadership that the conquering Vikings practiced. So they asked the Varangians to come, supposedly saying, "Our land is great and rich but there is no order in it, come and rule over us."

Another explanation is that the Varangians conquered the Slavs. Whichever the case, by governing the eastern Slavs' territory, especially Kiev, the Varangians controlled the Dnieper.

Varangian Trade Routes

In the 9th and 10th centuries the Dnieper River was the main trading route between the Baltic and Black seas. The Varangians, who were renowned shipbuilders and navigators, made Kiev, through which the Dnieper flows, their main trading center.

Once a year a major Varangian trading expedition would set off from Kiev southward for Constantinople. In the Byzantine capital the Varangians would exchange their furs, slaves, honey, and wax for wines, silks, and naval supplies.

In addition to Constantinople the Varangians also traveled east across the Caspian

Sea to trade with Persia and the wealthy city of Baghdad. With the Persians they traded Persian glass, Chinese silks, spices, and silver. Another prized commodity was amber, and the Varangians were eager to acquire as much of the precious material as possible.

Right: *An idealized view of the walled city of Constantinople, from a 15th-century illustration.*

The Birth of Dazhbog

Many cultures have myths about rites of passage, which include sons battling their fathers. This Slav myth is one of those, with the young Dazhbog fighting his father, Perun.

PERUN WAS THE SUPREME god of Kiev and the ruler of thunder and war. He lived with the other deities in Iriy, the kingdom of the gods. Tall and strongly built, like a champion warrior, Perun had long black hair and a thick golden beard. When he rode through the sky in his burning chariot he carried a flaming bow and a quiver of arrows to strike his enemies. When he journeyed through the forest he threw his thunderbolts to keep the wild animals at bay. Although Perun was a mighty god who could destroy the harvest in a single moment with a raging storm, he also controlled the gentler rains that watered the great Russian steppes and gave life to the grain.

One day the mighty Perun was walking on the bank of the Dnieper River. On the other side of the river he could see some pretty girls dancing and singing. One of the girls, Ros, was particularly beautiful, and Perun fell in love with her at first sight. He wanted to cross the river to try to get as close to Ros as possible, but the river would not let him cross.

Perun took his golden arrow and shot it across the river to where Ros was standing. The arrow flew across the river as fast as lightning and hit a large rock. The arrow caused the rock to glow brighter and brighter, until gradually a fire image of a man appeared on the stone. Perun called out to Ros to ask Svarog the creator for help. Ros did as Perun told her and called out for Svarog, who appeared by her side. He helped her to make a man out of the stone. That man was Dazhbog.

Dazhbog grew up to be a wise and fearless warrior. His fame and reputation spread all across the land and soon everybody had heard of him. One day when Perun was out walking he too got to hear about the strong and brave Dazhbog. Curious, he decided to seek him out.

Eventually he found Ros, who told him to go to a field where he would see his son, Dazhbog, playing. Perun went to the field and there for the first time he saw his son, playing with a cudgel (a small but heavy club). Then Perun challenged his son to a fight so that he could find out how strong his son really was.

Perun and Dazhbog started to fight — although Dazhbog did not know who he was fighting — and they fought for three whole days and three whole nights. They fought so hard that the earth

Above: *Perun, the god of thunder and war, and his son, Dazhbog, were often depicted as mighty warriors.*
This ancient stone relief of two warriors was found in the Balkans, a southern European region of Slavic influence.

screamed and the sea roared and the woods shook. Finally, Perun started to weaken and before long he fell down, unable to fight any more.

Dazhbog asked him who he was and Perun replied, "I am Perun, son of Svarog and come from the shining Iriy." Dazhbog immediately apologized to his father, saying, "Sorry dear father, I did not realize it was you."

Dazhbog went to see his mother and asked her if she would let him join his father in Iriy, the kingdom of the gods. Ros agreed, and Dazhbog went with his father to join the other gods in Iriy.

Vladimir's Pantheon of Slavic Deities

Unlike the Greek and Roman gods, the Slavic gods did not have a strict hierarchy. In general, however, most ancient Slavs saw five or six gods as more important than the rest.

Above: Domovoi *are spirits who live only in the house and can provide protection for the family. When one of the spirits feels displeased with the family he will knock over things in the house.*

Dazhbog, the god of sun, was one of the most important gods in the Kievan Rus pantheon and many stories about his life were told by the early Russians as they sat around their fire hearths in Kievan Rus. Kievan Rus was unique in the Slavic world in that it had a hierarchy of deities and statues symbolizing the gods. Although many of the gods and spirits were similar throughout the major Slavic cultures, each group, subgroup, and village had its own variation of the Slavic belief system.

The ancient myths of the Russian Slavs centered on their environment. They believed that every aspect of their world was imbued with a spirit that could be either peaceful or violent. The gods they worshiped represented different aspects of nature.

When Vladimir I took control of Kievan Rus in around A.D. 980, he erected statues of five or six major gods on a hill outside Kiev to mark the occasion. Historians think these statues were of Perun, Khors and/or Dazhbog, Stribog, Simargl, and Mokosh.

ROLES OF SLAVIC GODS

Chief of these gods was Perun, the god of thunder and war. Perun's statue had a wooden body with a silver head and a golden mustache. Often likened to the Scandinavian god of thunder, Thor, who carried a stone hammer,

Perun carried a battle-ax, a spear, and a club. When Perun was angry, the Slavs believed, he sent down powerful and bright bolts of lightning.

The son of Perun was Dazhbog, the sun god, who was particularly revered because the sun was treasured by the Slavs, who spent much of the year in darkness. Historians think Stribog was the god of winds. Mokosh is thought to have been the goddess of fertility and was later embodied in Mother Earth (also known as Moist Mother Earth, see page 44). She was the only female god and deeply respected because she was seen as the source of food. Little is known about Simargl or Khors, except that Khors may have been a variation of Dazhbog.

OTHER GODS AND SPIRITS

Other Slavic gods that were not included in Vladimir's pantheon but were worshiped by the Kievan Rus included the god of cattle and war, Volos (or Veles). His exact role is unknown, but he was identified with Perun, and soldiers would pray to both Volos and Perun before going into battle.

In addition to the gods, Slavs throughout central and eastern Europe believed in a spirit world. Animism — the belief that a spirit existed in

Above: *This folk-art painting on a box for face powder shows a young girl who is being called by water spirits.*

Below: *Wooden carving of a* rusalka *from a farmhouse.*

every animate and inanimate object — was powerful in the Slavic world. Slavic peasants depended on nature for their well-being, and the vagaries of the weather had a huge impact on whether they ate and kept warm.

Every action was influenced by a spirit. Every house had a spirit. Known as *domovoi*, these spirits were often the souls of ancestors. It was believed the prosperity of the household depended on keeping these spirits happy. Every river and body of water had a spirit, called *vodyanoi*; these spirits were old, ugly, and covered in slime.

Deep under the water lived water spirits called *rusalka*, who were sad because they were the souls of dead babies or drowned girls. The forest spirits known as *orleschi* were mostly malevolent, as were the spirits of the farmyard, the *dvorovoi*.

In order to keep all these spirits happy, Slav peasants had to make offerings and follow specific rituals.

The Marriage of Dazhbog

The warrior Dazhbog had many adventures and marriages. In this myth his marriage to a female warrior, mightier than he, brings sunlight to the world.

ONE DAY DAZHBOG was walking across a big field when he saw in the distance a warrior wearing the shiniest armor he had ever seen. The warrior rode on a large muscular horse with a long flowing mane. As he got closer to the warrior he realized that underneath the glistening armor was a young, beautiful woman.

Dazhbog, although dazzled by the appearance of the woman, decided that he would test her strength. He marched up to the warrior, pulled out his sword, and struck her. The woman warrior did not flinch but kept on riding. Dazhbog ran after her and hit her again. Still she did not move. "Who are you?" yelled Dazhbog, who was impressed by the young woman's strength. She replied that she had thought she was being stung by flies and was surprised to see that Dazhbog was actually a warrior.

Then, in the blink of an eye, she grabbed hold of Dazhbog, threw him into a crystal casket, locked it with a silver key, and attached it to her horse. The female warrior mounted her horse and galloped away. She rode for three whole days until finally her horse pleaded with her, "Brave and strong Zlatogorka, daughter of Vij, excuse me, but I cannot carry two warriors another step." Zlatogorka had forgotten all about the warrior in the crystal casket.

Taking pity on her horse, she released Dazhbog. Then she told the warrior that he must marry her; if he refused she would slay him. Dazhbog, blinded by Zlatogorka's beauty and awed by her strength, agreed to marry her.

Instantly, they ascended to the heavens, where they married. At first they were happy together. Then one day when they were out riding their horses they found a strange tomb. Written on the tomb was an inscription that read, "The one who lays in here will always stay by the rule of Fate."

Zlatogorka asked Dazhbog to try the tomb, but it was too small for him. No matter how he twisted his body he could not fit into the space. Then Zlatogorka tried and she fit the tomb perfectly. "Dear husband," she said, "put the cover on the tomb because I want to lie in here for a while." Dazhbog did as she asked and went hunting for a while. When he returned and tried to lift the lid off the tomb, it would not budge. Dazhbog tried everything. He hit the tomb with

Above: *Dazhbog gave light to the world by heating his cudgel before handing it to King Vij. For the Slavs scenes such as this misty morning sunrise through a Russian forest would not have possible without the warrior.*

his cudgel but nothing happened. Then he hit it with his sword and still nothing happened. The tomb's lid was stuck fast.

Zlatogorka called out to Dazhbog to go to her father, King Vij, give him her bow, and ask his forgiveness because, due to her foolishness, she had to stay in the tomb forever. Dazhbog went to the king and explained what had happened. Vij thought for a moment that Dazhbog had killed his daughter and demanded Dazhbog's cudgel. Dazhbog made his cudgel red-hot, then gave it to Vij. The red-hot cudgel brought light to the world, and Vij forgave Dazhbog and his daughter. Zlatogorka rested in peace from then on.

Marriage and Death in Pagan Russia

The different stories about Dazhbog and his various marriages underline the importance of marriage to the Russian people. The story of Zlatogorka and the tomb also introduces another important subject, death.

Weddings and funerals shared many similarities. Slavs viewed life as a cycle. Indeed, they compared life to an ear of corn, which grows from a seed in the earth and then returns to the earth. They believed that each person comes from his or her parents and ends life by returning to his or her parents in the ground, the womb of Moist Mother Earth. Weddings, too, were part of life's cycle and celebrated with the same fervor as funerals.

Wedding celebrations were only held once all the crops had been harvested in the fall and winter, and the party celebrated both the marriage and the gathering of crops. When Slavic peasants married each other in pagan times the wedding service varied from community to community.

Right: *A 17th-century Slavic dowry box, which would have been given by the bride's family to the bride's new husband.*

However, every community made sure that they took measures to prevent the wedding and marriage from being "spoiled." There were many rituals to protect the bride, particularly, from the devil, or Satanail (see page 10). In some villages, on the eve of the wedding all the windows and door of the bride's house would be shut to stop evil spirits from entering.

The best way to safeguard the wedding was to invite a known sorcerer to the wedding and give him the place of honor. This both placated the sorcerer and got him to help if needed. (It was believed that when devils or evil spirits married witches their weddings were often celebrated at a crossroads. The dancing became so frenzied that it raised a column of dust that reached the sky.)

FUNERAL CEREMONIES

At weddings, there were always lots of songs. Funerals also were seen as an occasion to sing. Death was not to be feared but to be celebrated as a rite of

Above: *A 19th-century painting titled* Sorcerer at the Peasant Wedding. *The practice of inviting the local wizard to a wedding went on well into the Christian era.*

Right: *This early 20th-century photograph shows two eastern Slavs wearing traditional funeral costumes.*

passage. The songs celebrated the relationship between the peasants and the land and praised their gods.

Early Slavic society was made up of a clan of both living and dead people. The dead were venerated, as minor gods, with the chief ancestor as the *domovoi* of the living (see page 21). The elders determined the values of their clan. They believed that each person was not a child of heaven but the fatherless son of the earth. This meant that all Russians were linked to each other and to all of humanity.

After death, they thought the soul embarked on a long journey for which it had to be made ready. The family had to leave open the windows and door so that the soul could leave. Then they prepared all the things the dead needed for the afterlife, including food, tools, clothing, and, in some cases, their wives, slaves, and horses too. The funeral banquet and ceremonies would last for several days.

Dazhbog and the Sorceress Marena

One of Dazhbog's marriages was to the evil witch Marena Svarogovna. Although she tried to kill the warrior, Dazhbog got help from some unlikely friends.

ONE DAY DAZHBOG WAS walking in Iriy, the kingdom of the gods, when he came across a large golden palace from which came beautiful music. Wondering who was making the enchanting sounds, Dazhbog entered the palace and followed the echoes of music and laughter until he found himself in a huge banqueting hall where a feast was taking place. At the head of the table he recognized the sorceress Marena Svarogovna. Then he realized that this was her palace. All his life his parents had warned him never to go there.

Marena knew who Dazhbog was and that his father was Perun, the god of thunder. She offered Dazhbog food, but he refused, thinking it might be poisoned. After the feast, Marena tried to lure the young warrior back to her private rooms, but he fled from the palace.

When Dazhbog's father, Perun, found out where his son had been, he was very angry and told him never to go near the sorceress again. His mother also scolded her son for being so reckless. Dazhbog, however, refused to listen to his parents' warnings and returned to Marena's palace the next day.

Marena was throwing another feast. Dazhbog entered the banqueting hall and shot a golden arrow into the air. When Marena's guests complained, he threatened to shoot them to pieces. Marena decided she had had enough of Dazhbog's bad behavior, so she turned him into an ox and let him loose in a field.

A few days later some shepherds who had been at the feast saw the ox and recognized that it was Dazhbog. They guided the ox to Perun and explained to him what had happened. Perun rewarded the shepherds for their kindness. Then he went to see Marena to persuade her to lift her spell. She agreed, on condition that Dazhbog wed her. Dazhbog had no choice but to marry the sorceress.

After the wedding Koshchei the Deathless, who abducts fair princesses, was jealous and sent evil spirits to destroy Dazhbog. For three days and nights Dazhbog fought the spirits before he finally defeated them. Exhausted by his trials the young warrior fell asleep. While Dazhbog slept, Koshchei persuaded Marena to run away with him.

When Dazhbog woke he realized Marena had gone. For weeks he searched everywhere trying to find his wife. When he finally met up with Marena

Above: *Even though Koshchei the Deathless was a close companion of the evil Marena, he was still able to feel pity for the brave Dazhbog. In this illustration from 1936, Koshchei is shown with his characteristically long fingers.*

and Koshchei they gave him wine to drink, which made Dazhbog drunk. Marena then ordered Koshchei to kill him while he slept, but Koshchei refused because he was no longer jealous of the warrior. When Dazhbog woke, Koshchei promised to give him three chances to escape.

The first time they threw Dazhbog into a deep well. Dazhbog's horse let down his tail, and the warrior climbed out of the well. He continued to chase Marena and Koshchei and again found them and drank the wine that made him drunk. But Koshchei still refused to kill Dazhbog. So Marena nailed her husband to a large rock.

Later that same day, Zhiva, the daughter of Svarog, king of heaven (see page 6), turned herself into a dove and while flying around saw Dazhbog. She fell in love with him at first sight and told him he had to forget Marena because she was evil. Dazhbog agreed, and the dove freed him from the rock and flew him back to Iriy.

Sorcerers and Witches

Like shamans in cultures throughout the world, sorcerers performed a vital and positive role in Slavic village life. But sorcerers were also to be feared and never made angry.

Below: *Russian sorcerers, or shamans, from the 19th century.*

In Slavic mythology and folklore there are many stories about magicians. Sorcerers like Marena Svarogovna (see page 26) were a crucial part of daily life for Slavic peasants. As recently as the 19th century, rural Russians relied on sorcerers for advice and protection as much as they did on their local priests.

The sorcerer was consulted on all matters of daily life — birth, marriage, and death — as well as daily events.

People believed that their local sorcerers — be they witches or wizards — held the key to keeping both evil and good spirits in check.

Every Russian village had its own sorcerer. His responsibilities were great, but his main job was to use spells to ward off evil spirits. Although the sorcerers were respected, they were also feared, because the villagers believed they not only had the power to cast good spells but also evil spells if they were displeased or angered.

EVIL SPELLS

When anything bad happened, the villagers usually blamed it on a spell cast by the sorcerer. Any event, such as accidents or neighbors becoming angry with each other, was blamed on a sorcerer's spell. It was believed that a sorcerer's magic could be transmitted secretly through any means, from food and drink to clothes and small animals. It was also believed that sorcerers could change into birds or animals.

Every major and minor disease or illness, such as epilepsy or even hiccups, was thought to be an evil spirit in the body placed there by a sorcerer. People also thought that wizards controlled the wind and that witches stole dew and rain, which explained why there were droughts.

Sorcerers could also perform good and useful deeds, such as looking into the future and deciphering the hidden meanings of omens. Such talents made them extremely powerful in the village, and until the Christian priests arrived, the sorcerer was the most important person in the village.

The connection between sorcerers and devils was very close. When Kievan Rus converted to Christianity in the 10th century, the first priests battled to stop rural communities from consulting sorcerers. It took centuries before the Christian priests succeeded in convincing the local people that they should be relied on for daily and spiritual matters, and that sorcerers should be mistrusted.

People then started to protect themselves against witchcraft and the sorcerer's powers. They believed a stove-rake, suspended over the cottage door, could prevent a wizard from entering, and crosses were placed inside the home to stop witches from getting in.

Vlad the Impaler

Thanks to the late 19th-century novel *Dracula*, by British writer Bram Stoker (1847–1912), and to numerous movies in the 20th century about the notorious count, the myth of the vampire proved the most famous to come out of the Slavic region. Legend has it that Stoker based his creature on a real 15th-century ruler of Walachia, in present-day Romania, named Prince Vlad Tepes: The prince was also known as "Vlad the Impaler" because of the way he executed his prisoners. But the vampire myth actually began with the early Christian priests who tried to convert the Slavs. They claimed that anyone who was "unclean," such as criminals, heretics, and sorcerers, did not rest in death but turned into the living dead, sucking human blood at night and turning their victims into vampires.

Left: *A portrait of Vlad the Impaler, the inspiration for* Dracula.

Dobrynya the Dragonslayer

Like Dazhbog and other Slavic heroes, Dobrynya represented highly valued qualities, such as bravery and honor in battle. This tale is one of the warrior's most famous adventures.

ONE DAY THE brave Dobrynya came home to find his mother very upset. She warned him not to go to his favorite places — the river and the mountains — because the evil she-dragon was living there. A long time before, the brave Dobrynya had slain the offspring of the she-dragon in revenge for her kidnapping people from Kiev.

Ignoring his mother's advice, Dobrynya decided to swim in the river next time he went there. As he dove into the water he saw a tongue of fire licking clouds of smoke. Out of the flames emerged the 12-headed she-dragon. She recognized Dobrynya immediately and threatened to swallow him. But Dobrynya was too quick and dove under the water.

Dobrynya swam as fast as he could to get away, but the dragon jumped into the water after him and had almost caught up when Dobrynya spied a priest's hat in the water. He knew the hat would protect him against the dragon so he held it up to her head. The dragon cowered as Dobrynya drew out his knife to kill her. The cunning she-dragon pleaded with Dobrynya to spare her life in exchange for not killing any more Russians.

Dobrynya hesitated for just a second and the dragon seized her chance and flew away, taking with her Dobrynya's horse and weapons, leaving him with nothing. Dobrynya had no choice but to walk all the way back to Kiev, which took a very long time. When finally he got back to the city he discovered the dragon had kidnapped Prince Vladimir's favorite niece, Zabava. Everyone loved Zabava and was very upset. The prince decided that only Dobrynya could save his niece and ordered him to find her.

Dobrynya returned to his mother, dejected. He did not know how he could fight the might of the she-dragon — he had no weapons or horse to fight with. His mother told him not to worry. He was to take his father's horse.

The horse was very old. For the past 15 years it had been living in the stable. But Dobrynya trusted his mother, so he did as she said.

The next morning, as he saddled the horse, his mother gave him a gift, a magic silk whip that he was to use when the horse seemed tired. Dobrynya set off and rode for days and days until he reached the land of the dragons. As far as the eye could see there were dragons fighting Russians. Dobrynya

Above: *This lacquered box shows the hero Dobrynya battling a dragon. Colorful re-creations of the tale and other adventures of Dobrynya were common in Russian folk art.*

fought lots of battles and released many of the Russians the dragons had captured. Eventually his horse tired and seemed incapable of continuing. Dobrynya brought out his mother's gift and tapped the horse on his back with the silk whip. Instantly, the horse's energy returned.

Finally, Dobrynya came face to face with the evil she-dragon. She refused point-blank to return Zabava. For three days and nights Dobrynya and the dragon fought. Just when Dobrynya was about to collapse from exhaustion

he heard a voice speak to him from the heavens. The voice told him to be brave and keep going for another three hours, after which he would be successful and defeat the evil she-dragon.

Dobrynya did as he was told, and after three hours he killed the she-dragon. He then found Zabava, put her on the back of his brave horse, and rode with her to Kiev. When they arrived in the city there was much rejoicing at the princess's safe return and the slaying of the dragon by the brave hero Dobrynya.

Early Christianity in Kievan Rus

For the eastern Slavs living in Kievan Rus, Christianity came in the 10th century. Christianity in Russia, as in other places in the world, adopted some pagan aspects of the old culture.

The story of Dobrynya and the dragon (see page 30) has elements of both Christian and pagan influences, which was common in Russian history tales. The brave Dobrynya, for example, was one of the legendary heroes of Kievan Rus and was claimed to be the uncle of the ruler Vladimir I (about 956–1015), who imposed Christianity on his subjects in A.D. 988. Dobrynya was also identified with Saint George, the Christian dragonslayer.

Just eight years before the introduction of Christianity in Kievan Rus, Vladimir had erected statues to honor the pagan gods on a hill outside Kiev (see page 20). When he converted to Christianity he had the statues dismantled and thrown into the Dnieper River while his subjects wept.

Vladimir's reasons for converting to Christianity were mostly political. At the time the German states were threatening Kievan Rus, and Vladimir sought the aid of the Byzantine

Left: *This 19th-century painting titled* Baptism of Russia, *by Viktor M. Wasnezov, gives a romantic view of Vladimir I overseeing the conversion to Christianity of the eastern Slavs.*

Empire. The Byzantine emperor, Basil II (976–1025), agreed to an alliance on condition that Vladimir convert to Christianity. He did, but while the tiny aristocratic elite who lived in Kiev accepted Christianity, the rural peasants — the majority of Kievan Rus's population — were reluctant

converts. It was not until the 19th century that Orthodox Christianity became the dominant religion.

At first peasants refused to abandon their pagan idols because they believed the gods, who must be kept happy through regular worship, were solely responsible for the earth's fertility. But when they were forced by the government and the Church to convert to Christianity, the peasants appeared to worship the Christian God and saints while really praying to their pagan gods. Over time the two religions merged in the minds of the peasants, in what is known as double faith, or *dvoeverie*.

DOUBLE FAITH

Double faith existed in many places throughout Europe. New Christian festivals were often held on the day of an earlier pagan festival. The date of Christmas was taken from the pagan calendar, for example.

Left: *As Christianity and paganism merged in double faith, Dobrynya was transformed into the Christian Saint George, shown slaying a dragon.*

Below: *Built entirely of wood, the Church of the Intercession is typical of Russia's early churches. Worshiping indoors was a new experience for the Slavs, since pagan worship was performed outside.*

Over time, pagan gods transformed into Christian saints. The Slavic god of cattle and war, Volos, became Saint Vlas; Moist Mother Earth was worshiped as Saint Paraskeva; and Perun, the god of thunder and war, was eventually prayed to as Saint Elijah.

An important aspect of the pagan religion was the telling through myth of how the Slavs' world came into creation. As new saints and heroes were introduced to their pantheon, the peasants worked them into their traditional stories. The story of Dobrynya, for example, was transformed into the Christian story of Saint George the dragonslayer.

Not all aspects of pagan worship transformed into Christian worship. Before the 10th century, pagan rituals were often held under oak trees. The pagans did not build formal places of worship. Christians, however, built hundreds of churches, many of which still stand (see page 37).

Sadko the Minstrel

Sadko's journey to the bottom of the sea is similar to the ancient Greek myth of Orpheus in the Underworld. A major difference, however, is that Sadko's tale has a happy ending.

THE MUSICIAN SADKO earned his living by playing the gusli (an ancient Russian musical instrument similar to a zither) for guests at the banquets of rich merchants.

For a while he had no work. One day, feeling depressed, he walked aimlessly until he reached the shore of Lake Il'men. There he played his gusli all day long until, in the middle of the lake, a huge wave appeared. Scared, Sadko ran home.

Still without work, Sadko returned to the lake the next day and the one after that and played his gusli. On the third day, as he plucked the strings of his instrument, out from the depths of the lake emerged the sea god.

He thanked Sadko for his beautiful playing and said he wanted to reward him. The sea god told Sadko that the next day he would be invited to play at a rich man's banquet where the guests would boast about their wealth.

Sadko was to say nothing until they finished boasting, then he should bet the merchants that golden fish lived in the lake. If he won the bet they would have to give him their shops.

Sadko did just as he was told. Each time the merchants put their nets into the lake, they pulled out a golden fish. From that day on Sadko the minstrel was a very rich man.

One day, returning from a long and profitable sea voyage, his ship loaded with precious metals and jewels, Sadko and his men found themselves marooned when the wind dropped. Hours passed without any wind.

Sadko realized he must make an offering to the sea god of one of the crew. Each man, including Sadko, threw a twig into the sea. When Sadko's twig sank he knew he must be the sacrifice. He jumped into the water, sad that he was leaving behind all his wealth.

When he awoke, Sadko found himself in the palace of the sea god at the bottom of the sea. The god was angry with Sadko for his lack of gratitude and told him he must stay and play his gusli.

For many days Sadko played and played. One day, an old man appeared and told Sadko to do just as he said and he would be set free. The old man told Sadko to take a wife, to marry her but not to touch her on the wedding night. Sadko followed the old man's instructions exactly and woke up to find himself back in his village with his new wife and his wealth waiting for him.

Left: *A 19th-century painting, by Ilya Repin, showing Sadko in the underwater palace of the sea god. The minstrel is surrounded by beautiful maidens.*

Life in Kievan Rus

As one of the most important cities in 10th-century Europe and as a major trading post on the Dnieper River, Kiev had a distinct social system that spread across Russia.

Left: *This mid-19th-century painting shows a typical Russian village at midday. Rural life in Russia changed little from the 10th century to the early 20th century.*

When Sadko the minstrel won his bet (see page 34) he became extremely wealthy and joined the elite of Kievan Rus society — the merchants and princes who ruled the city of Kiev. Kiev's strategic position on the Dnieper River, with its access to the trading posts of Constantinople in the south and the realm of the Varangians to the north, brought great wealth to the city. However, only a few enjoyed the wealth because it stayed in the hands of the merchants and princes.

Most people were farmers who lived in rural communities outside Kiev in the forests and swamp lands. The peasants raised crops, such as wheat, millet, rye, garlic, cabbages, and turnips, and kept cows, sheep, and pigs. To add to their diet, they hunted, fished, and kept bees for honey. The peasants were poor and only had the land that they farmed, which they passed on to their sons.

The merchants called the peasants *smerdy*, which means the "stinky ones." Whether this referred to their lack of bathing or their garlic breath we do not know. The peasants could not read or write. The little free time they had was spent at celebrations for weddings and funerals, dances to celebrate successful harvests or just listening, during the

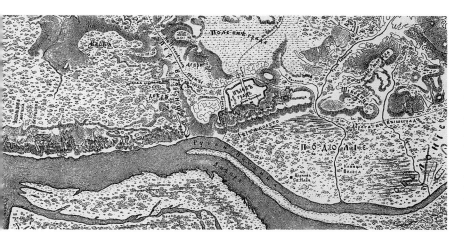

long winter nights, to the many myths and legends that were passed down from generation to generation.

In Kiev, the princes employed a group of officials, known as *boyare*, to administer the state. At first, the officials had no contact with the farmers, but gradually they started to rent out equipment and small pieces of their land to peasants. In return, the peasants had to repay the loan, and before long they fell into debt.

Above: *A 19th-century repro-duction of a 9th-century map of Kiev, the center of Kievan Rus, the first Slavic state.*

This was how the process of serfdom, where the working class was forced to farm for wealthy landowners, started. It lasted until the 1860s.

LIFE OF LUXURY

While life for the rural peasants was to remain unchanged for centuries, during the heyday of Kievan Rus, life for the princes and merchants was one of luxury. The merchants were often also warriors who had to protect their trade routes from attack. Their trade included precious stones and metals, wine, furs, honey, and grain, which they exchanged for spices and metals. They lived in palaces in Kiev. A popular way of demonstrating their wealth was to hold banquets where minstrels, such as Sadko, would play.

Saint Sophia Cathedral

Kiev, which was a city and a state, was one of the powers in Europe when Vladimir I converted to Christianity in the late 10th century. Soon afterward he began an aggressive program of building large cathedrals, until the city had more than 400. Cultural and religious life in Kiev flourished as the Russian Orthodox Church, as the eastern Slav branch of Christianity became known, spread its influence. For example, Saint Sophia's Cathedral, built between 1017 and 1031, had the first school and first library in the city. Some of the original structure survives today.

Left: *The cupola in Saint Sophia's, built in Kiev in the 11th century.*

Ilya Muromets and the Giant

Ilya Muromets became the model bogatyr, or Slavic knight. His bravery and skill in battle served as inspiration to Russian warriors for centuries.

WHILE THE PARENTS of Ilya Muromets worked hard in the fields, Ilya sat alone in their cottage doing nothing. All his life he had done nothing because his arms and legs were paralyzed. His days were spent waiting for his parents to return home to care for him.

One day, while his parents were busy making haystacks, Ilya was, as usual, alone in the cottage when three wayfarers stopped by. They asked Ilya to get up and give them a drink. "Happily I would give you a drink, but I cannot move," Ilya explained. They ordered him once again to get up. This time, Ilya stood up as if he had always walked.

He gave the men a drink, and they told Ilya to take a sip. As he drank his whole body strengthened and he felt he could do anything. The men told him to drink again, and this time he felt half his strength disappear. The visitors told Ilya he would be a great hero who would win many battles, but first he had to buy a foal and travel to Kiev, where he was to make the city his home. Before the wayfarers departed they gave him some advice — never fight the giant called Svyatogar.

Ilya went to the field where his parents were asleep, exhausted from their work. Ilya took pity on

them and finished the haystacks. When they woke they were amazed. Ilya told them what had happened and that he must move to Kiev. Although his parents were sad that their son had to leave, they helped him prepare for his journey. He bought a foal, as instructed, which he fed well for three months. Then he slept for many days and nights.

Ilya was awakened by his young horse. The earth was shaking as the mighty giant Svyatogar approached on his giant horse. The giant was so tall that when he sat on his horse, his head touched the clouds. On his right shoulder he balanced a crystal casket. When Svyatogar reached the oak tree where Ilya was hiding he dismounted and opened the casket. Out stepped the giant's beautiful wife.

Svyatogar then sat against the tree and napped. Meanwhile the giant's wife put Ilya into the giant's pocket so he could join them on their travels. A few hours later the giant woke, replaced his wife in the casket, mounted his horse, and set off again.

He had not traveled far when his horse complained of the extra weight. Much to his surprise, the giant found Ilya in his pocket. Angry with his wife, Svyatogar killed her. He then

Above: *Ilya Muromets, the Slavic hero knight, in the tree, and Svyatogar, the giant, on his horse. The tales of Ilya Muromets were popular among the Slavs for generations and promoted positive values of bravery and honor.*

dragged Ilya to the Holy Mountains. There, they found a tomb, too big for Ilya but a perfect fit for the giant. Ilya warned Svyatogar not to get in, but he refused to listen.

Trapped in the tomb, the giant asked Ilya to release him. He tried everything but nothing worked. Then, the giant asked him to blow on the tomb, saying he would give Ilya all his strength. Ilya refused, saying he was strong enough. The giant told Ilya to take his sword and leave. Svyatogar stayed in his tomb forever, and Ilya became a mighty warrior who won many battles.

Hero Knights of Early Christian Russia

The bogatyri, like King Arthur's Knights of the Round Table, had many heroic adventures, but they also gave Slavic men a central role in the once female-dominated society.

The peasants' son Ilya Muromets (see page 38) was one of the most admired of all the early Slavic heroes. There are many different stories of his adventures, but they all stress common features, particularly Ilya's bravery and loyalty — characteristics that Ilya shares with Perun, the god of lightning.

Ilya Muromets is the most famous of Russian heroes, or *bogatyri*. Bogatyr

Above: *This 19th-century painting shows, from left to right, Alesha Popovich, Ilya Muromets, and Dobrynya as* bogatyri. *The artist was Viktor Vasnetsov.*

means "champion," and the word only came into Slavic use after Christianity was introduced to Russia in the 10th century. A *bogatyr* was a knight of Holy Russia and a good Christian.

There are many different epic poems that tell of the *bogatyri*'s adventures. The *bogatyr* could come from any walk of life and was linked to a specific place. Many of these champions came from Kiev, including Ilya, whose final act was to build Kiev Cathedral, and Dobrynya the dragonslayer (see page 30). Sadko the minstrel (see page 34), another kind of *bogatyr*, was connected with Kiev, Novgorod, and the Volga River.

SAVIORS OF RUSSIA

After Christianity had become well rooted in Russian life, the peasants worshiped the knights as demigods because they fought God's enemies, the evil spirits and demons sent by the devil, or Satanail. The stories recounted how the brave warriors defended

Left: *The famous Russian illustrator Ivan Bilibin published this book of* byliny — *tales of the* bogatyri — *in 1904.*

Kievan Rus from the many aggressive nomad tribes, such as the Polovtsians and Pechenegs. These constant invaders came from Asia along the southern steppes with the aim of seizing control of Kiev.

The knights usually appeared in so-called "wonder tales," but their adventures were also told in other types of Russian legends, particularly the epics — or *byliny* — which were part of early Russia's oral tradition. A key aspect of these stories was the mixing of pagan elements with Christian belief. Scholars think that the stories were created by priests as a way of blending the pagan gods with Christianity (see pages 32–33).

Women of Kievan Rus

With the arrival of the *bogatyri* life for women in Kievan Rus changed dramatically. In pagan Russia, fertility was prized above everything else, and female deities, such as Moist Mother Earth, were revered. The strength of women was reflected in the many pagan stories where women such as Vasilisa and Baba Yaga (see page 42) played a central role. With the advent of Christianity, women's position in society began to weaken and the increasing popularity of the *bogatyri* allowed men to take center stage in society. Men's cultural importance increased too, taking over women's traditional place at the center of Slavic mythology.

Above: *This giant statue of Mother Russia, in Kiev, can be thought of as a symbol of the important place women have held in Slavic society.*

Baba Yaga and Vasilisa

The story of Vasilisa combines elements of Cinderella, *with its evil stepmother*, and Hansel and Gretel, *with its wicked witch.* In this tale, Baba Yaga, the witch, actually helps the heroine.

WHEN THE MERCHANT'S daughter, Vasilisa, was eight years old her mother died. On her death bed, Vasilisa's mother gave the young girl a doll that would always protect her. A few years later, Vasilisa's father remarried, and Vasilisa now had a stepmother and two stepsisters. But Vasilisa's father quickly regretted the marriage because his new wife was a nag who was eager to spend all his money. Also the stepsisters did not like having to share things with Vasilisa and grew jealous of her.

One day, when Vasilisa's father was away on business, her stepmother moved the three girls deep into the forest to stay in an old cottage. Vasilisa's stepmother deliberately extinguished all the fire for cooking and light in the house and ordered Vasilisa to go to Baba Yaga's cottage nearby to get some more. Baba Yaga was an old witch. It was said that she ate people, especially little girls.

Vasilisa set off through the dark forest. She was frightened, but the magic doll, in her pocket as always, told her not to worry. Nevertheless, the young Vasilisa grew increasingly scared, especially when dawn broke and a horseman, dressed all in white, thundered past her. As Vasilisa walked on deeper into the forest, another horseman, this time dressed in red, rushed past.

Finally, Vasilisa reached Baba Yaga's cottage. Its fence was made of human bones and skulls with glaring eyes on top. As night fell Vasilisa saw that the skulls began to glow. Suddenly another horseman, in black, flew past, followed quickly by Baba Yaga herself. The old witch was riding a worn-out broomstick that glided through the air like a bird. The little girl was frozen with fright.

"I smell Russian blood," screeched the witch. Vasilisa could not hide and explained to Baba Yaga that she needed some fire. The witch agreed to give her some in exchange for some tasks. But if Vasilisa did not do them properly, then Baba Yaga would eat her.

Her first task was to prepare dinner. Baba Yaga ate enough for 10 people; the few scraps she left Vasilisa fed to her doll. The next day, Baba Yaga gave her many new tasks before going out for the day. The doll did all the jobs while the witch was out. When Baba Yaga got home, she gave Vasilisa even more jobs for the next day.

When she got home the next day, Baba Yaga found the cottage neat and tidy and the food well

Above: *Baba Yaga was a complex witch who could be both evil and good. This illustration of the witch appeared in a book of old Russian tales in 1915.*

prepared. "Why don't you speak?" roared the witch to Vasilisa, who replied she had one question. "Who were the riders?" she asked.

"They are the day, sun, and night, and I control them." Baba Yaga was pleased Vasilisa did not ask any more, so she let Vasilisa go home, carrying the fire in a skull. As she walked home Vasilisa thought that she should throw away the skull, but the skull sensed the little girl's thoughts and told her not to.

Back at the cottage the skull burned down the place, killing the wicked stepmother and her daughters, leaving only Vasilisa and her doll. When Vasilisa's father returned he was happy to have his beloved daughter all to himself.

Female Deities and Fertility Rituals

Before the Slavic conversion to Christianity, the goddess Mokosh was one of the most important deities, and women were responsible for performing many sacred rituals.

In ancient Russian myths Baba Yaga is often portrayed as an evil witch who steals and eats children in her cottage deep in the forest. But she has another side, that of a maternal and protective mother. In many stories about Baba Yaga she does not ride an old broomstick (see page 42) but flies on a pestle and mortar. This symbolizes the two sides of Baba Yaga, because she uses the pestle and mortar either to destroy her enemies or to fertilize the earth.

Baba Yaga's ability to create life parallels that of the only female god in the Kievan Rus pantheon, Mokosh (see page 20–21). Mokosh is the goddess of fertility. Since her name means moist, she has been linked with the most revered of ancient Russia's cults, the earth.

The early Slavs worshiped the earth, calling it "Moist" or "Holy" Mother Earth. The worship of Moist Mother Earth eventually turned into the worship of Saint Paraskeva, a Russian

Left: *For Slavic peasants, the pagan goddess Mokosh became the revered Russian Orthodox saint Paraskeva, shown here in this 17th-century painting about the saint's life.*

Orthodox saint, and the Virgin Mary. The peasants believed the earth was responsible for every stage of life — it gave birth to the crops and received the bodies of the dead. Farmers also believed that Moist Mother Earth could tell them whether it would be a good harvest or not.

MOTHER EARTH RITUALS

There were many rites that showed how the Slavic peasants revered the earth. For example, during certain times of the year it was believed that the earth was pregnant with crops and could not be hit. If, during this time, children hit the ground with a stick even while playing, their parents or the village elders would scold them saying, "It is a sin to beat the earth, for she is our mother."

A pagan ritual that existed well into Christian times was practiced whenever sickness struck any of the villagers or farm animals. The women of the village would go to the fields at midnight to plow. They would strip to their underwear and let down their hair under the night sky. Some of the women pulled the plow, while the others howled and banged sticks on pans. Then they dug a furrow around the village which, they believed, released Moist Mother Earth's healing

Right: This early 19th-century painting titled Grain Harvest, *by Aleksei Venetsianov, depicts the idea that women and the earth, as bearer of food, are connected.*

Below: A Russian folk art painting of a young woman, perhaps performing the traditional fertility dance.

powers to fight the evil that had caused the illness.

Peasants also performed rituals for the earth every August. They took a jar of hemp oil into a field where they said prayers in the four major directions — north, east, west, and south — pouring a little oil onto the ground. They bowed to the rising sun in the east and asked Moist Mother Earth to keep evil spirits in check. Bowing to the west, they asked her to use fires to destroy evil. To the south, they asked for southerly winds to prevent bad weather, and to the north, they asked the earth to protect them from bad weather. At the end of the ceremony they smashed the jar of oil on the ground.

Glossary

animism The belief that life exists in all animate and inanimate objects, and that people have souls.

Baba Yaga An evil old witch who eats children, but is sometimes portrayed as maternal and protective.

Basil II The emperor of Byzantium who convinced **Vladimir** to convert to Christianity.

bogatyri Legendary Slavic hero knights, similar to King Arthur's Knights of the Round Table.

Bogomils A popular Christian movement between the 10th and 15th centuries that emphasized the battle between good and evil.

Byelobog The Slavic god of light and good.

byliny Russian epic poems that emerged from of the Slavic oral tradition and often featured **bogatyri**.

Chernobog The ancient Slavic god of night and evil.

Constantinople Capital of Byzantium, also called the Byzantine empire, and a major trading partner with the city of Kiev.

cudgel A small, heavy club used as a weapon.

Dazhbog Originally a **Scythian** or **Sarmatian** sun god, adopted by the Slavs as their own sun god and warrior hero. Also the son of **Perun**, the god of thunder and war.

Dnieper A river in Russia. In Slavic mythology he becomes a river mightier than either of his two sisters, **Dvina** and **Volga**.

Dobrynya One of the most popular Slavic hero knights, or *bogatyri*. Famed as a dragonslayer, he became identified with the Christian saint George.

domovoi Spirits that live in houses, and are usually the spirits of the family's ancestors.

Drevlyáne People who lived in the Russian forests.

Dvina A river in Russia. In Slavic mythology she, along with her sister **Volga**, tried to become a mighty river before her brother **Dnieper**.

dvorovoi Spirits that live in farmyards.

Iriy The kingdom of the gods.

Khors One of the gods included in **Vladimir**'s pantheon of gods.

Koshchei the Deathless An evil spirit who abducted princesses and was a close friend of **Marena**.

Marena A mighty sorceress who married **Dazhbog**, but after the wedding tried to get **Koshchei** to kill him.

Mokosh Also known as Mother Earth or Moist Mother Earth, and the only female deity included in **Vladimir**'s pantheon of gods. She was later identified with the Christian saint Paraskeva.

Muromets, Ilya One of the most famous *bogatyri*. The stories of his adventures and his bravery and honor in battle inspired generations of Slavs.

orleschi Spirits, usually dangerous, that inhabit the forests.

Perun The god of thunder and war, and the father of **Dazhbog**. He is based on the Viking god Thor.

Polyáne People who lived in the Russian steppes.

Prav The path of what is morally right, as created by **Rod**.

Rod A god who emerged, with the help of Lada, goddess of love and springtime, from a golden egg and created the universe and most everything on earth. He also separated the physical world from the spiritual world.

Ros The mother of **Dazhbog**.

Rurik of Jutland A 9th-century **Varangian** prince who began the expansion of Varangian rule over the eastern Slavs, before the occupation of Kiev.

rusalka Sad spirits that live deep under water and are believed to be the souls of babies or drowned girls.

Sadko the minstrel A musician, like Orpheus in Greek mythology, who had many adventures, including journeying to the kingdom at the bottom of the sea.

Sarmatians A nomadic people who, like the **Scythians**, originated in Iran; they took over the Scythian empire in southern Russia in around the 4th century B.C.

Satanail The pagan Slavic version of the biblical Satan.

Scythians A nomadic people who originated in Iran and traveled to southern Russia between the 8th and 7th centuries B.C.

Simargl One of the gods included in **Vladimir**'s pantheon of pagan gods in Kiev.

Saint Sophia's Cathedral Built in the 11th century, for centuries it was Kiev's most important cathedral.

Stribog One of the gods included in **Vladimir**'s pantheon of gods. He may have been the god of winds.

Svarog The son of Sva (the spirit of **Rod**), he became the king of heaven and ruler of the gods, and finished the creation. He was also the father of **Zhiva**.

Svyatogar The mighty giant who captured **Ilya Muromets** but ended up trapped in a tomb, thus freeing the hero knight to go on to have many adventures.

Varangians Vikings who settled in territories occupied by the eastern Slavs and ended up ruling over them.

Vasilisa A girl forced by her wicked stepmother to get some fire from **Baba Yaga**'s cottage. With the help of her magical doll, she earned the witch's respect, was freed, and burned to death her stepmother.

Vladimir I Ruler of Kievan Rus in the late 10th century who was responsible for converting the Slavs in the region to Christianity. Before his conversion he built five or six statues in Kiev, each representing a different member of the pantheon of pagan gods.

Vlad the Impaler A 15th-century prince of Walachia, in present-day Romania. His methods of torture and cruelty toward his prisoners were legendary, and in the late 19th century British author Bram Stoker used the prince as the inspiration for the title character of his novel *Dracula*.

Volga A river in Russia. In Slavic mythology she, along with her sister

Dvina, tried to become a mighty river before her brother **Dnieper**.

vodyanoi Spirits that live in water and springs and appear old, ugly, and covered in slime.

Volos Also known as Veles, god of cattle, he was closely identified with **Perun**. After the Slavs were converted to Christianity, he was transformed into Saint Vlas.

Yav The path of what is morally wrong, as created by **Rod**.

Zabava The niece of **Vladimir**, she was rescued from a 12-headed dragon by **Dobrynya**.

Zhiva The daughter of **Svarog**, she freed **Dazhbog** from the large rock where **Marena** had tied him.

Zlatogorka The female warrior who married **Dazhbog**. She ended up trapped in a tomb.

Further Reading & Viewing

BOOKS

Afanasyev, Aleksandr Nikolaevicher, et al. *Russian Fairy Tales*. New York, NY: Random House, 1976.

Avery, Gillian. *Russian Fairy Tales*. New York, NY: Everyman's Library, 1995.

Barrett, Tracy. *Anna of Byzantium*. New York, NY: Laureleaf, 2000.

Forests of the Vampire: Slavic Myth and Mankind. Alexandria, VA: Time Life, 1999.

Mayer, Marianna. *Baba Yaga and Vasilisa the Brave*. New York, NY: William Morrow & Co., 1994.

McNally, R. T., et al. *In Search of Dracula*. Boston, MA: Hougton Mifflin, 1994.

Phinney, Margaret Yatsevitch, et al. *Baba Yaga: A Russian Folktale*. Greenvale, NY: Mondo Publication, 1995.

VIDEOS

Byzantium: The Lost Empire. Discovery Home Video, 2001.

Dracula: Fact or Fiction. Republic Studios, 1993.

Dragons: Myths and Legends. A&E Video, 2000.

Russia. Questar, 1995.

WEBSITES

Mything Links: Pan Slavic Tradition and Beliefs. http://www.mythinglinks.org/euro~east~panSlavic.html.

Rambaud on the Kievan Rus in the Pre-Christian Era. http://www.shsu.edu/~his_ncp/PagKiev.html.

Index